The Metamict State

University of Central Florida
Contemporary Poetry Series

The Metamict State

. . . an unusual state of matter, amorphous be-
cause of the disruption of the crystal structure
by radiation from contained or nearby radio-
active atoms.

Roald Hoffmann

Cover illustration by A.R. Ammons

UNIVERSITY PRESSES OF FLORIDA
University of Central Florida Press
Orlando

8 11.54
H67m
1 4 6535
may
1989

Library of Congress Cataloging in Publication Data

Hoffmann, Roald,
    The metamict state / Roald Hoffmann.
        p. cm. — (University of Central Florida contemporary
    poetry series)
        Subtitle: —An unusual state of matter, amorphous because
    of the disruption of the crystal structure by radiation from
    contained or nearby radioactive atoms.
        ISBN 0-8130-0869-7 (alk. paper)
        I. Title. II. Series.
    PS3558.03468M48   1987
    811'.54—dc19   87-17621
                                                         CIP

University Presses of Florida is the central agency for scholarly publishing of the State of Florida's university system, producing books selected for publication by the faculty editorial committees of Florida's nine public universities: Florida A&M University (Tallahassee), Florida Atlantic University (Boca Raton), Florida International University (Miami), Florida State University (Tallahassee), University of Central Florida (Orlando), University of Florida (Gainesville), University of North Florida (Jacksonville), University of South Florida (Tampa), University of West Florida (Pensacola).

Orders for books published by all member presses should be addressed to University Presses of Florida, 15 NW 15th Street, Gainesville, FL 32603.

The cover is a black-and-white version of a watercolor by A.R. Ammons.

Acknowledgments

The author gratefully acknowledges the publications that first published the poems listed below:

"Cosmetic Company Buys Eisenhower College," *Michigan Quarterly Review*, vol. 24, no. 2 (1985).
"The Devil Teaches Thermodynamics," *Webster Review*, XI, 2 (Fall, 1986).
"From Lake Louise," *the new renaissance*, vol. VII, no. 3.
"In an Antique Shop in 's Gravenhage," *kentucky poetry review* (fall 1987).
"Mind Grackles," *Gryphon* (1987).
"Napkin Engineering," *Manhattan Poetry Review*, vol. 4 (1986).
"New Traffic Patterns Ahead," *Negative Capability* (1987).
"Next Slide Please," *Aldrichimica Acta*, vol. 19, no. 1 (1986).
"Touching the Surface," *New Letters*, vol. 53, no. 2 (1987).
"Men and Molecules," *Synthesis*, vol. 7, no. 1 (1984).
"Finnair Fragment," "From a Rise of Land to the Sea" in *Songs from Unsung Worlds*, B. B. Gordon, editor, Birkhäuser, Boston (1985).
"Three Japanese Edo-Period Pots," *Vienna Review* (1985).
"An Unusual State of Matter," *Bound* (1986).

For my mother, Clara

Contents

I

The Devil Teaches Thermodynamics

My second law, your second law, ordains
that local order, structures in space
and time, be crafted in ever-so-losing
contention with proximal disorder in
this neat but getting messier universe.
And we, in the intricate machinery of our
healthy bodies and life-support systems,
in the written and televised word do declare
the majesty of the zoning ordinances
of this Law. But oh so smart, we think
that we are not things, like weeds,
or rust, or plain boulders, and so
invent a reason for an eternal subsidy
of our perfection, or at least perfectibility,
give it the names of God or the immortal
soul. And while we allow the dissipations
that cannot be hid, like death, and—in literary
stances—even the end of love, we make
the others just plain evil: anger, lust,
pride—the whole lot of pimples of the spirit.
Diseases need vectors, so the old call
goes out for me. But the kicker is that the struts
of God's stave church, those nice seven,
they're such a tense and compressed support
group that when they get through you're really
ready to let off some magma. Faith serves up
passing certitude to weak minds, recruits for
the cults, and too much of her is going to play
hell with that other grand invention
of yours, the social contract. Boring
Prudence hangs around with conservatives,
and Love, love you say! Love one, leave
out the others. Love them all, none will love

you. I tell you, friends, love is the greatest
entropy-increasing device invented by God.
Love is *my* law's sweet man. And for God
himself, well, his oneness seems too
much for natural man to love, so he comes up
with Northern Irelands and Lebanons . . .

The argument to be made is not
for your run-of-the-mill degeneracy, my
stereotype. No, I want us to awake,
join the imperfect universe at peace with
the disorder that orders. For the cold
death sets in slowly, and there is time,
so much time, for the stars' light to scatter
off the eddies of chance, into our minds,
there to build ever more perfect loves,
invisible cities, our own constellations.

Touching the Surface

The concrete lies in reeds, green
wart head just above water.

What makes it lie still may be the abstract,
a hypothesis of a thousand enzyme

factories churning bonds, pieces
of a good meal, or just the notion

of satiety. It watches, this barely
breathing concrete, at eye-water

level still other parts of its extended
self. . . . mosquito larvae pushing

their snouts through thick skin water,
whirligigs' random skim. The abstract

weaves theories around this scene:
it notes the absence of shadows

towards night, surface tension,
the possibility (the abstract

is hardly ever sure) of a chemical
repellant excreted by these flitting

beetles; how nice it might be to tie
a fly joining essences of larva

and whirligig, the food search
pattern in that skim, species

altruism, why so many eggs laid
by a mosquito. The abstract

watches; the mind, easily distracted,
blinks, and the bullfrog, reaching

for what one must be one with, leaps.

Flag of Poland

1

We enter
or have always been
in this room
whose corners congeal
only when we look for them.
An experiment is in progress,
but it is uncertain
if we are in control
or just observers.

A woman stands quietly with me.
Before us
spotlit on a platform of gray stone,
with fossils in it,
the soft cream coil of a ptarmigan or swan.
It can barely lift its head.
From the dark rises the taut and killing
        head of a red snake,
but it's also weak
and falls back on the bird's contour feathers.
I see the snake's tongue flicker
and we sense
its intent
to strike
and sink fangs into the bird's neck.

It would do so instantly,
except that both are cold. But we
do not feel the cold.
And now we remember,
or always knew,

that we
or others behind some partition
can tune this cold.
There is ice under the platform.
The snake changes to a lizard,
rears up, falls back
closer to the snow goose's neck.
The bird only swivels its head,
eyes on the red.
The lizard is now a lion totem
jammed into the slim snake skin.
Its claws are pressing out.
There will be blood.
The reds will clash.
I can't stop it.
The snake-lion pounces.

2

Men caught me in the rushes
and cut my wings. They think
innocence into my whiteness.
I must play their role. But
oh this quiet radiating cold
penetrates the down, my skin,
worse than the blizzards I
hid through on my island. This
cold, it is his way of making
me weak and submissive. And
the danger of that red weaving
sting, too close to my warmth.
Why do they want me killed?
Let me move. It is his dream,
but she looks at me. They can
turn the cold off, and the snake

of their Garden of Eden will
kill me.

I was a red wave over roots
and stones, and I took the scuttling
brown vermin of the forest floor.
When I had need of them. Not
in fear, like men with boots
and sticks beating the bushes
for me, afraid of my image
within them, afraid of themselves.
But now they have forced me through
some crack of time, willed me
next to this life in white feathers.
Whose life—hers, theirs together?
I must reach the bird's head—the man wants
me to, even if I feel no hunger.
But then he sends me the essence
of winter, to pull me back
to the vaguely remembered
creeping in under rocks, to curl
on dry leaves in my own circle
of near sleep. And when I
cannot resist the cold, he changes
me, as he cannot change himself.
A snake-lizard-lion pupa
I rise to strike.

I am the silent watcher,
the woman moving in and out
of the shadow he creates. He
makes me the perfect bystander,
with the semblance of control.
He doesn't let me cry,
or say this experiment
must end. I look good
in white. I am afraid.

3

The cold slows but cannot stop
the final weave and snap.
Blood drops down the feathers,
as little absorbed as water would be.
And the bird's circle unfolds
to show its feathered feet.
I half wake, toss
to redream that ending.

4

The snow goose wakes,
it is not her dream.
She rises, fluffs herself.
There is a smell not of the tundra,
which makes her move out of the light.
But the snake follows,
quick, ready to jump . . .

5

The lion metamorphoses again, moves in.
I call to the engineers in the booth
to turn on more cold, to stop him.
They are slow,
talk of response time.
There is no time.
There is too much time.
The snake-lion kills
me, alone, into the morning.

Self-Edge

1

Shell, husk, bark, tank armor,
carapace. There are softer
machineries of protection:

A finger tip tracks the cream
paper trim of a sheet of
commemoratives, each flashy,

engraved clone set patient
in inner processions of per-
foration, inkling of a ripping

apart future. The rim:
a squarish ambulatory
bearing occasional

plate numbers, admonishing
messages to use zip codes,
the color proofs of whatever

rotogravure press spit
this sheet. If not frayed
in handling, the selvage

is abandoned, torn off.
Turning the sheet over
you see the slick trace

of a mind or machine that
had hoped for more: the gumming,
all the way out to the edge.

2

My taste runs to textiles. So
you proffer alternative
saving means: In the hem

of a Shirvan carpet, weft
doubles back over the twinned
warp, securing its own

return. Or, in afterthought,
the body of the rug plenty
supple and done, you loop

and twirl around, over and
over the long edge warp
thread. A binding, in toned

indigo, of survivor soul
into this runner. At the short
ends cotton fringes serve.

3

But what if shuffling
time, dirt, the intrusive
heels of others act to fray

off all the throw-away
hulls and wrap we built on?
The true edge sharp

exposed, a threat of total
unraveling. Nicks grow
into crevasses, wild

stressed rips cut in
and through a structure
that small energies saved for a while.

Mind Grackles

We are circling, we are flying,
beating novice wings, not
in sky's jig, not in courting
darts, but
        g-forces gentled,
plying earnest updrafts
for lift. It isn't easy
this flying, for something must
be forced past, something
molecular, and we must learn
to curl our wings just right,
so that which passes
                passes
overwing, and part of us is always
falling, and part sucked up
by this fraction less of nothing
streamed by, a fast pull past,
a draw up to the sky. Feathered
airfoils bend, the wing is wind.
Flying
        is a kind of balanced
falling,
        out of the blue-black
squawk of us, into the by,
a slip of deeply forked tails,
a shift, askew, a swing.

One for Bishop Berkeley

Zoom
the lifeless stretch
to Orion, searching, scanning
all the way, then
back through where we are,
plunge
reeling out this or that measuring tape
into submicron oscillations
of enzymes' inanimate girders.
Separate 'scopes are conscripted,
micro and tele, for out
is far, and one must reach
the cavities
where the tiny structures hide.

So, in bits, we sketch in
this escalator of powers of ten.
Stuck in the middle, a life
of delimited sizes, child's 4
to my $16^{1/2}/32$.
And even then one sleeve always too long.
Count in the intestinal flora,
a right whale,
and still the sentient
crowds on a few steps.

Wouldn't it make more sense
to have us top the master plan?
Biggest is best, not only in squashes
at the 4-H Fair, and if all devolved
from us, fell in threads below,
ah, then we could rest, secure
in our creation, we unnervous gods,

and having built in a random number
generator, for we'd want the small
things to run occasionally counter
to our plan, we'd sit and watch,
on our eternal picnic, all
that fuss and fun below.

Or, tiny but elemental clusters
freed of doubt of our divisibility,
we would reproduce, willfully,
stack, aggregate, grow
effortlessly upward, the only way
for us. We'd make use of the chance
turns of nature for color, softnesses
and shapes. In time
green vines would come, climbing
trellises of our own making.
Nothing insecure, or uncanny,
for the atoms that we are
would be in all.

But in the middle
is where the brain
is,
constrained
by the skull,
bound
by stretched skin,
few slits
for the senses to flow through.
So this transforming prisoner
beams out, thinks:
See it big
the stars
make them far.
See it small
a cell.

Querying
the proximate causes
of its confinement,
testing powers,
dreaming,
it strews the world
with all the sizes of its creation.

New Traffic Patterns Ahead

Let me eat the crumbs off your muffin
darling,
    let me try
    to simplify
my life. I'm tired of pavlova
and kiwi,
    tongue in jelly
    vermicelli
plain vanilla's what I need,
just like they show it on TV.

Let me eat the crumbs off your muffin
baby,
    drop deluxe
    sell the tux
real cheap. I'll slip on my western gear,
brass buckle,
    Springsteen's
    pale blue jeans
country music's in town and you've
got piles of that NEH money.

Let me eat the crumbs off your muffin
honey,
    no more of
    Raskolnikov
He's dull; I've taken up computer
science. You
    know the Mac's
    got sexy syntax
So let's move to Tulsa; you can teach
a course on Yeats and Ammons.

II

Three Poems from Japan

1. *Akihabara*

In this quadraphonic, centibel town
there is a warren of roads,
of electrified covered arcades,
Akihabara.
Tokyo's discount mart of electronic gear.
A babble and babel of brand names:
>   Teac, Sony, Yaesu
>   Panasonic, Nakamichi, JVC

Escalators couple the stores,
stacked like amplifiers in lab racks.
Speakers, shrouded, reach to the ceiling.
Litany of buttons, controls, meters,
head phones, batteries, and switches,
Hi-fi's oriental, super-occidental El Dorado:
>   Teac, Sony, Yaesu
>   Panasonic, Nakamichi, JVC

Akihabara
You are a contemptuous advertisement of our riches,
with your feed-in receptacles, grounded plugs.
Your life-blood, the wastrel, giver of shocks,
courses in braided copper wires, in plastic sheaths.
Your collapsible ears, antennae attuned to the aether.
And your eyes—you have no eyes. . . .
You have digital meters and LED displays.
You have no eyes.
>   But what a mouth!
Muzzled with screens, but full of shriek.

Akihabara
Take your music which I, addicted, desire,
take your Russian and Swedish shortwave programs,
radio clandestine Zimbabwe,
your news and gray weather,
bedded in commercials, like cheap sushi
I'm going to turn you off.

2. *Bunraku*

Three black-hooded manipulators,
one fragile many-hued puppet.
One man moves the left hand
one moves the robe, simulating invisible feet
one does the rest, a lot.
In an alcove to the side
the chanter bawls news of war,
receives death, plots revenge.
The samisen player squats to left.

Three hooded men, one puppet.
Three move, the puppet's free.
    No Balinese shadow play, finger puppet, or
        marionette.
Control's explicit, and thereby vanishes.

In the catacomb theatre of my dreams
you, dear lady, are a puppet too.
You bear your father's wind-creased face
    and his gall too.
Your husband's sex-ridden carapace supports you,
your teacher's goads hold your mask in place.
But, to your lovers you are more than real.
They see beauty, elegance, wit
and for the brief impassioned moment
in which they are drawn near
their eyes perceive no hooded movers.

3. *Japanese Science*

The only rickshaw I saw, hooded with brocade,
had a geisha in it.
And the old tattered man who pulled it
chattered incessantly.
The curtain stirred, flashing a pale painted face.
And the man's feet clapped as he dodged the cars.
To a rich man's party, no doubt.
Yes, here come the black rented limousines,
white doilies on their back seats.

A red lacquer box, Kamakura ware,
hides in its polished perfection
the place where it opens.
No hinges, just a perfect fit.
And on the black and shiny inside
field, a straw and a solitary
golden cricket, imprisoned.
The man I knew in Sendai,
master of his western equation-soaked trade,
divided space into fundamental unit cells.
He claimed, deductively, to be able to
build from them the cricket's chirp and
geisha's paint.
A powerful methodology, his.
But I think he just built more perfect boxes.

From 12,000 Meters

These are the Siberian tundra's waters:
Oxbow moons in the tangled
    tributaries of the Yenisei;
And sheets of glistening lakes,
    a giant carp's scales caught in the sun.
Further, lakes rounded to machined perfection.
    Are they meteor craters, or
            some ancient earth lord's
                    communion wafers?
They are covered with ice.
And it is only September!

Finnair Fragment

Ice berglets, poked down
by my oil rig stick
in Iittala's fluted glass
fail to break the
roiled golden mirror
of jazzy bubbly, covering
a fleeting rift
of the laws of physics.
They really do like ice here. . . .
Rise, perforated cubelets,
relent, let Archimedes
rest in peace.
Or have you, polyvowelled friends
conspired in brief white nights
to make a truly light champagne?

From a Rise of Land to the Sea

The water's shore-lapping signature
is a random drone, picking a
wet string of nature's scrapping still
moments. Sun-freckled wavelets dive.
Yawl rubs against buoy, teased
to a sporadic dulled tinkle that
rises over the wind in the
lindens. The same wily actor
folds the feel of the sea gently
into my back, drives the clouds.

The multisensual mixing is darned good, my engineer,
        my director.
You even provide low comedy in a pesky fly and drama
in the jet swish of a swallow diving to her
eaves nest that I, intruder here, obstruct.

Eva at Skogshem

In the season of content, when yellow
linden surplices of scent surround a buzz
of swirling bumblebees, I, pilgrim-like,
traverse this globe-lamp-lined path. I
have been here before. Half my life
ago, twenty-two years old, I walked to
Löwdin's summer school. And, being early, waited
by that bench, by roses midst the gravel,
a weathering statue of Pan. You came
into my life then. With simplest English, a smile
turned in time to limpid love. It was the
seed crystal of our life, it was summer too.
Oh, Eva, I still see your blue and white blouse.

Bicycling on Lidingö

This gray cycle is a step-through model;
in the U.S. we'd call it a girl's bike.
A foot brake, no speeds, my son would sink it
in the ground with his ten-speed derailleur
contempt. Yet it rolls, or bounces, through bikeways
of conscientious Swedish planning, it winds
along paths of asphalt and level dirt,
sun spokes falling on wayside blueberry
and lingon bushes. It wheels past rust red
houses with white trim, pristine bays flashing
by the trees. Night sun of midsummer melds
pine and birch to the yellow side of green
steering the sky into a Swedish flag.
The path moving, the bicycle stands still,
I think I saw a fox along that hill.

In an Antique Shop in 's Gravenhage

I met the proprietress
        by asking, as I often do,
for a Victorian jelly mold.
Plump, jangling keys, somebody's grandmother,
she came to the door.
Listened, and in a voice
        accented softer than a silk scarf
            she said:
        "No, I know what you search,
but none has come my way for years.
Look around, meneer.
You may find what you desire.
        I have my tea."
And swayed through a curtain.

The shop was cluttered with majolica plates,
bisque one-eyed dolls lacking hair,
Chinese ceramic dogs,
tarnished copper coins.
A wooden plane, rusted on edge.
I heard her tea things clatter,
        a slight whiff of fresh tobacco added
            to the Victorian must.

In cases lay ivory belt buckles
stamped "Souvenir de Sénégal,"
ladles and prints of Frisian fishermen,
scrimshaw and polished beads,
an infinity of cups.
        I sidestepped a dark desk, and saw
        two rocking chairs needing caning
        cradling satanic andirons.

I was ready to leave. No sound
came from the back room
        "Thank you, and goodbye," I said,
banging the door handle.
        But a draft caught me,
billowed out the printed curtain,
        propelled me to see her.
Closing the half-opened door
        I went back,
knocked on the dark frame,
        parted the curtain:

Neat space
confined by bureaus and mirrors
reflecting the source of the breeze—
        an open window.
On the enameled table a teacup,
        half a sandwich,
        a tuliped vase, beige doily,
        a cigarette on a sculptured ashtray,
        smoke still rising.
But nothing of her.
I closed the curtain and left.

Of such moments is life.
The screeches forgotten
        the occasional true silences
                etched in.
Mysterious details may be manufactured
in the telling. No matter—
        for me:

Mevrouw will take her amber
tea with cress sandwiches, she'll
wear necklaces of sea lion teeth,
midst Lalique vases,
        midst chiffoniers.

Then she will vanish
            not into haze
            not into crowds
but into the receptive keep
of my imagining mind.

Entwined

For the draft from your horn
they would kill you. But
on the weavers' red ground
you are safe. Oaks rise

like fountains encircled
by flower clumps from lost
pattern books. They think you
tamed . . . I am to teach

you music, so next I practice
the organ lesson, my
servant abstracted
at the bellows. You hear me,

breathe in tact, you are
too still. In another
scene I braid a garland
and you hold the standard

caparisoned, redundant
in the colors of the house
I must marry in. They will
have me wear strict clothes

too. You watch the monkey
sniff at a flower filched
from my basket, you smell
the morsels parakeets,

rakish hares eat. White
flanks shiver, but the intent
horn is steady, pointing.
"Well trained," the beaten hunters

whisper to each other; so you
don't cringe as I reach my hand
for the cubit-long, scribed
horn, in another tapestry.

The last tapestry
is unwoven:
In it, night fades the red ground
and cats' eyes glare in the bush.
I lie, still,
wanting your
unreality
to enter me
make me
pale
as the aurora,
to slip past castle doors,
guards, wedding feast,
to pass their gray time.
Come real, be me!
The hares sleep.

From Lake Louise

Darkness ascends, caught
in the mountain bowl.
If this mirroring lake
can invert glaciers, flip
moraines deftly up
gravity's chute, can
it deny me the loner's
spring of desire, to impel
my word past these cliffs
to newly blinking Sirius?
How else can I reach you?
The intent of love travels
at superluminar speed;
its ray reflects, making
you, two thousand miles
away, you who stand in
the driveway, having forgotten
to turn on the garage
lights, lift your eyes
to meet the selfsame
lord of the star-brood,
my messenger.

Young Whiskey Jack

You seem to ascend straight
from the turquoise lake deep
below us both, up an angled
straight line that threatens,
for you loom larger, but do
not span space. Settle in the
snow that lifts itself in tiny
creaks from the larch needles
below. The sun warms this south
exposure. I strew sunflower
seeds too salty for me, worry if
they may harm you, but give in
to the need you have of me.
You eat them all. Fly
to the top of a dead tree, shift
to a compromise log, then
to an inch of my still boot.
The seeds are gone. All is
surveyed, nothing left but
to explore with a sideways
flick of your gray and white head
this dangerous, dispensing human
bulk, spread the tail feathers,
peep up here, and off
to the golden larches
which love you
but do not feed you.

Toledo

1

Meeting place of earth and sky . . .
and of all those who fell here
by that finely struck local steel
in the hands of others—Iberians,
Visigoths, Moors, Jews, Castilians,
Nationalists, Republicans. I think
how their souls, once loosed, would
rise in unpropelled swaying, gently,
knowing that gravity must not pull
them down any longer, missing it.
The way to nothingness is only up, but
this hard blue dome of the southern
sky confines. They bounce, in
eerie suspension of the freedom
granted, bob back up, searching
for the funnel, the nexus, the passage.

2

This is one. Crimped by the bend
of the Tagus and the clay-baking
sun, the sun which pries open canyons,
heats brown hills, the rocks upon hills,
goats wandering in the brush. The eye
makes a small trespass to a pin-prick
pattern of distant olives, dissolve
to fields, mauve rocks breaking
through the same difficultly
tillable earth. To the west a live
strip of green, river darkening life.

3

The way up is the town: gray
and red stone and plaster,
boulders bracing this mountain
of shards and earthly offal,
walls upon crumbling walls, tiled
patios in narrowing streets. Hung
between the poles of the Alcazar
and the Cathedral, the city mounts
to meet a sky that spreads,
cloudlessly focussed by this crag
of a settlement. Toledo—
hard lessons on how the
solid meets the light.

4

The Cretan, Domenikos Theotokopoulos,
came late here, after Visigoths and Arabs.
His Venetian apprenticeship done, he paints
saints, the descent from the cross,
commissioned portraits of cardinals.
And in a church, friends mourning the Count
of Orgaz, in their lace-fringed tunics,
in brocade, fine court dress. Above . . .
the swirl of robes of saints, converging
to sweep us up to a still unseen third
world. But not with ease; we see
long bodies stretching to leave earth,
keeping their elongation of excess
desire even as they bend to help others
raise themselves. To the light above! Their
sinews, bone, hard and soft trappings
of robes and body tensed in too much

light: El Greco felt the nexus and stayed
in the city. He also painted it in a storm.

5

The Primacy of Spain: the glittering eagle
of a lectern, candles and the tinkle
of hidden nuns can't dispel the spacy
murkiness of this Cathedral.
But the chancel! Pierced by light,
a high passage to the sky, ascendant,
fringed by figures of a rich tribe.
We are in a well, under impossible
ice. They must see us, these ornate
angels, patriarchs of the Transparente.
They fish for us. One even lowers
a lamp in outstretched hands. Who
is holding him? To the light
their flaming grace pulls us on up.

6

Their temple gone, the speech of the Jews
to the one God rose in unprepossessing
synagogues of brick and plaster.
In El Transito the lattice work lace
of alabaster, Mudejar arches rise
near the roof. Below, darkness, only
two circumambulating strips of golden
Hebrew. I make out words—the root of
praise, names of the Lord, blessings.
This is the fortress of perfect letters,
built by those who came with the Moors,
healed and studied and wrote love
poems in Arabic, and, in the year that Their

Catholic Monarchs felled the last Muslim
kingdom of Granada, in the year when
Columbus brought back from La Isla Española
the gold for a monstrance, in that
year of their Lord, the Jews
who did not convert were forced on
another upward, sideways, dispersing
journey—to the Rhine, to the other Galicia.

7

So the past is mustered
by the town; to tell
what it was to live
and be expelled,
leaving bones to replenish
olive fields; to praise
indifferent gods,
in black and white,
in darknesses whose need
is to be pierced by figured
shafts; with sounds,
the true sheen of cut;
to paint
the stretched thigh
of God.
These lopsided passions
the earth incites
and the city
stands
brazed and rising.

III

Men and Molecules

Cantilevered methyl groups,
battered in endless anharmonic motion.
A molecule swims,
dispersing its functionality,
scattering its reactive centers.
　　Not every collision,
not every punctilious trajectory
by which billiard-ball complexes
arrive at their calculable meeting places
leads to reaction.
　　Most encounters end in
a harmless sideways swipe.
An exchange of momentum,
a mere deflection.
　　And so it is for us.
The hard knock must be just right.
The eyes need lock, and
glimmers of intent penetrate.
　　The setting counts.
A soft brush of mohair
or touch of hand.
A perfumed breeze.
　　Men (and women) are not
　　　　as different from molecules
　　　　as they think.

Deceptively like a Solid

The conference is on Glass, in
Montreal. Wintry light declines
to penetrate windows, and soon
will be lit glass-enclosed glows
so that we may talk, talk into
the night (fortified by bottled
mineral waters), of the metric
of order trespassing on prevailing
chaos that gives this warder
of our warmed up air, clinker,
its viscous, transparent strength.

The beginning was, is
silica, this peon stuff
of the earth, in quartz,

cristoballite, coesite,
stishovite. Pristine marching
bands of atoms

(surpassing the names we give
them) build crystalline lattices
from chains, rings, of Si

alternating with oxygen,
each silicon tetrahedrally
coordinated

by O's, each oxygen
ion, so different from the
life-giving, inflaming

diatomic gas, joining
two silicons; on to rings
in diamondoid

perfection in cristoballite;
helical O-Si-O chains
in quartz, handed in

coiling, mirror images
of each other, hard, ionic
SiO_2.

There must be reasons for such
perfection—time lent to the
earth: then lava

flowed, the air blew thicker, still
no compound or simple eye
to fret defect

into the ur-liquid from which silica
crystallized. But in time we did
come, handy, set

to garner sand, limestone, soda
ash, to break the still witness
of silica. Heat

disrupts. Not the warmth of
Alabama midsummer
evenings, not your hand

but formless wonder of pro-
longed fire, the blast of air drawn
in, controlled fire

storms. Sand, which is silica,
melts. To a liquid, where
order is local

but not long-range. Atoms wander
from their places, bonds break,
tetrahedra

in a tizzy, juxtapose, chains tilt,
bump and stretch—Jaggerwalky.
The restive structures

in microscopic turmoil
meld to gross flow, bubbling
eddies of the melt.

Peace in crystal meshes, peace
in hot yellow flux. But the gloved
men who hold the ladles
get nervy volcanoes
on their minds. So—tilt, pour . . .
douse, so quench,
freeze in that micro lurch.
Glass forms,
and who would have thought it clear?

We posit that the chanced,
in its innards so upset, ought
not be transparent. Light
scattered from entangled polymer
blocks, adventitious dirt,
owes it to us—oh, we see it
so clearly—to lose its way,
come awash in black or at
least in the muddy browns
of spring run-off, another flux.

But light's submicroscopic
tap dance is done in place.
The crossed fields shimmer,
resonant, they plink
electron orbits of O and Si.
Atoms matter, their neighbors
less, the tangle of the locked-in
liquid irrelevant in the
birthing of color, or lack of it.

Optical fibers   Crystal Palace
      The Worshipful Company of Glass Sellers
recycled   Millefiori
prone to shattering   Prince Rupert's drops
Chartres, Rouen, Amiens   float
Pyrex   Vycor   glass wool
network modifiers   the Palomar mirror
smoked for viewing eclipses   thermos
lead glass   microcrack
etched with hydrofluoric acid   spun
frustration   bull's eyes   annealed
borosilicate   softening point

High winds on Etna or Kilauea
spin off the surface
of a lava lake thin fibers.
Pele's hair.
The Goddesses' hair,
here black.

Moon's Moonlets Gone

A satellite going round a planet has a lower and an upper region of stability. Below a certain altitude (called the Roche limit) a satellite, due to the strong tidal forces of the parent body, is torn to bits. Above a certain distance, the gravitational force of the parent body is so weak that any perturbation due to another object can jettison it from its stable orbit.

—*Science Age* (Bombay) 1, 79 (1983)

1

Out there at apogee, it's just a tumbling
to pass time in darkness. The hauling
in is by something too distant to mark

if it is hot or cold, planet or satellite.
It's a weak tie, too; the orbit's eccentric,
visitors, though few, come and go. There

is time to feel their draw, increment
to fade. In the fly-by, an exchange
of angular momentum so the next swing

out is further. A hazardous orbit glance
provides escape velocity, but one
doesn't know what one will be captured by.

2

Closer in, those body tides, pulls
on the solid . . . We're not talking of flesh
but what tugs true at earth. Not just moon's

hold on water, the scribbling of runes
in flotsam and seaweed, not the diurnal
loading and unloading, what timed

John Cabot's sail (at Avonmouth the spring
tide is 40 feet). The moon does her own
thing, but what we are after is the strong

craft that put a bulge on Mercury, that makes
a lady of the night keep her face on us
as we roll. A mighty inverse square slow

haul of the round and massive on what comes
near. Density matters. In the obsessive
limit we elongate the seemingly solid

smaller, and when the coherent forces
are beat, at Roche's limit, a couple radii,
the body—body that was one—gives.

3

But then what of those cones, stout bullets,
prong-like things sprouting antennas,
solar cell wings, in metal thongs (aesthetics

and aerodynamics don't matter up there),
what of those beeping artifacts we send up
with a flame, a sensor and hope?

Well within the limit, they don't break.
The earth yanks, the same silent pull. Nothing
gives. For a clever brood has welded in

strict joints, struts, tightened bolts. We're
good at holding things together. For
a while—other fiery frictions wait below.

4

What troubles we get in . . . and out.
Saturn's rings, a ranging orbit's gambit.
Best to sit still, but momentum

and gravity won't let you—there is push
and pull. Going's on, forever, not pained
by people unable to solve

explicitly, the three-body problem.

Next Slide, Please

there was no question that the reaction worked
but transient colors were seen
in the slurry of sodium methoxide in dichloromethane
and we got a whole lot of products
for which we can't sort out the kinetics
the next slide will show
the most important part
very rapidly
within two minutes
and I forgot to say on further warming
we get in fact the ketone
you can't read it on the slides
but I refer to the structure you saw before
the low temperature infrared spectrum
as I say
gives very direct evidence
so does the NMR
we calculated it
throwing away the geminal coupling
which is of course wrong
there is a difference of 0.9 parts per million
and it is a singlet
and sharp
which means two things
either
you're doing this NMR in excess methoxide
and it's exchanging
or
I would hazard a guess
that certainly in these nucleophilic conditions
there could well be
an alternative path
to the enone you see there

it's difficult to see
you could monitor this quite well in the infrared
I'm sorry in the NMR
my time is up I see
well this is a brief summary of our work
not all of which
I've had time to go into
in as much detail as I wanted
today.

Napkin Engineering

Imagine that we were not such soft flesh
that splits on rusted bolts and splinters,
but something harder, that takes a sheen.
And that the lymphs, puses, chaotic

fluids that course down metastasis
freeways, or in just messy plumbing
double-park residues at every bend, that
all the viscosity bled out. Imagine,

a better us, not some tinkerer-in-slime-
molds' body building exercise, but something
engineered to last: In shiny 304
stainless steel, or vacuum melt bar

stock, a complex of traps, chambers, pumped
down manifolds (no hardened arteries here;
at 10^{-10} torr a molecule can travel
a mile before side-swiping another). This

is the efficient concept, a two-piece
clamped body design, crevice-free butt
welds to reduce the risk of contamination,
flanged fittings, easier than nuts in tight

situations. Signals come through charged
mosaic membranes, there is bell-mouthing
for our beam and ion needs, to feed those long
cool laser jets coursing past gray pump

shrouds, passing chilled vanes, in dog leg
throttling curves' control; control, the computers
know it well. Energies need in and out, through
cooled orifice plates, reduced nipples. Custom

penetrations can be drilled on demand.
Mounting? In any position. Who needs
fantasy, this high on high vacuum.
The mechanism, self-lubricating bronze

nut of chips in the bonnet, can gate
the flux in a six-way cube cross, walk
the dog, hang the man. A speck of rust?
Imagine that! Abrade, ion gun at the ready.
Sputter up, sputter down—it's matter, thrust.

—With thanks to the exhibitors of equipment at the
32nd National Symposium of the American Vacuum
Society, Houston, November 1985

Searchers and Deciders

We begin by sampling, selectively
the excrescences of Nature's richesse
then willfully tune in on the coded beat

of her tinkerer's drum. To bind in the force
of a differential equation, to model,
            reduce . . . ah, that is power,

        control, and
                        in the end
            not too difficult,
for some of us,
            smart kids,
have learned our lessons well.

The patterns pulse on, to be revealed
to careful listeners in Osaka
and Heidelberg, as well as Ithaca.

So there we are, uncharismatic
heroes of the myth of progress
oh how we love to preen

before each other, in the finery
of our jargon, the intricacies
we trace in seeming chaos.

But the world has invented other
most needed players of the game,
shepherds of men and goods,

slaughterers, advocates and fighters.
They who choose the time

to heal or kill, compress

our knowledge to power their tools.
        Our tools.
They manage, in good will
                        and once
        in a while
                drop bombs
and kill sweet lakes too.

And if we think they rule
the world unwisely, I vouch
we'd do no better.

Some of the searchers have qualms:
Are we then at fault, for having
in our precision of the electrons'

perky dance in alloy lattices loosed into
the world the ken of beams, sheets,
tank wheels with which *they* weld

the world's doom? We posit, for
that is all we opt to do, that those
tunes and pirouettes of mind

and matter might have been
allowed to lie unformed, unmined
and we the better for it.

But no, no. The ur-secrets of Nature
don't lie there passively. They
grow into our minds like dandelions,

they strangle us with their imminence
and we in turn are Nature's
garden tool for their unveiling.

They will not be concealed.
And so . . . the feeders and the sellers,
the priests and governors, have

cast us players in a tragedy. In
holy madness fed by the weed of what
we learn, we learn, deprived of choice,

the things that may harm us.
It is our pain to know, to know,
the dewy glimmer
                    of the snake
fernshoot,
        as it unfurls,
                unhid,
                    to consume us.

To What End

On prolix days
I, diseased by infinity,
trundle fractions to their limit,
add a half to one, then a third, a fourth, a fifth . . .
the pesky, counterintuitive
divergence of it all.

I sunder line segments
into smaller ones,
carving out in each interval
a crisp crevasse of nothingness
for another, in-between to fall,
wedged secure by its neighbors only
until my next partition stroke.
There is no lasting togetherness for numbers.

In extension and intrusion
I look for the frozen moment
of reaching the end
(which is not an end)
to which all may be added,
and all is unchanged.

On such days I play
in endless poker games
where the stakes rise exponentially,
follow the horizons on every sphere,
and walk down railroad tracks
to prevent them from meeting.

But infinities are only theoretical
and terminate
in the limit
of the solitary
I.

Complaints against the Body, and Its Reply

I'm not old, but I know
a new joint will shift
into hurting gear every
winter—shoulder, knee, ankle—
will it be hip's turn next?
And when the acute pain
is done, traces, twinges return—
my body's private showing
of this feelie tape, newsreel
of my past and future
crimes against it.

I hate my body when it
fails me. I think
"This year I will run three
miles up Snyder Hill Rd. again"
and then a cartilage is torn
ignominiously, raking leaves,
a false mole hole step.
And every footfall thereafter
a pain-focus. Of course
I run on it, addict, and it
gets worse. "This year
I will ride again. Maybe
work up to polo." Under my
mind's touch the mare's flank
ripples with chestnut power,
but all I can do is to drink
in the stable smell.

I know I mistreat it.
I tear off toe nails when
I'm nervous, stopping

only at blood. Then I'm
impatient with their healing.
And don't stand me next
to the paté and shrimp
at receptions, because
I don't have your willpower
to move. I root there like
any pig. I eat and drink
in binges, sentenced to
measure out my fun by
the aftertaste of Rolaids
and the level of the antacid
bottle.

I am angry with my body.
Trivial pains, you say,
but I'm sure age has
more failures of marrow,
sphincter, artery to loose
than you or I wish,
clinically, to imagine.

So what does the defendant say to all that?

Bodies are bodies, an endless rhythm
of biochemical cycles nudged into
perfection, binding effortlessly
the vital component of the air
with the feed, the water, churning
them, chopping a bond here, never
too many, until the molecular
puzzle pieces are sufficiently
small, right to be built up by
noninfernal machinery, assembled
into the microscopic servants and
messengers of the organism—enzymes,
hormones, the stuff of genes, the machine

itself. Proteins—transparent as
in the marvelous eye lens, or red
as hemoglobin. In colors, shapes,
degrees of softness and hardness,
their small actions multiply
to extend the muscle, to give
the heart valve the motive
power to open as it must,
and, eventually, in coordination
to walk, stumble, and to recover
from that stumbling; to think,
ever so simply, to remember
poems and equations and Emil
Nolde's landscapes, the traces of love
and God, even to forget the body
that is around and with this brain . . .

So the body says: gurgle, thump-thump.
And when I think I am angry
with my body I mean: my mind
is angry with itself. Which
will not do. Only outsiders
can be blamed. We choose,
unfailingly, those
whom we love most.

IV

Admission Price

1

A push from the wild side,
is that what's needed?
To make plain words facet

being, skim to soar, to counter-
point world's inner and outer,
or just to carry a tune?

To do all that—must one run,
not walk, those razorback
ridges in and out of the fogs

of the sane? In the dips
or off barely hid edge—soul
mire, paranoia, smashed

bottles, whiffs of real opium,
seduction's rip pull. Giving in,
or lashing out (either way)

a spiral of darkening mind
coils to spring, free
poets in their youth. They sing,

yes say to life, in jerky march
to the alcoholic twin-barrel
shotgun, sleeping pill altar

of the savage god. And we can't
get their tune out of our mind.

2

Or, if not that death direct
then a kind of stretching
of a scream around sharp

corners. Must it be that?
Inside, the carom of un-
dissipated anger, caress

worn down, caring tough.
Worms, an upwelling of memory
to forced swallow of innards

and gristle, and milk scum.
Or worse: a child that wasn't.
Then things must out, it is time:

a pass through the crooked
neuron funnel that sublimes—
a change of form, a change

into words, transmitted,
transmutes. A shearing of desire.

3

In search of other gates:

I listen to: firecrackers for St. John's Eve,
   cows astray in the almond
   and olive groves: Mallorca.
I remember, in another place: the dead
   goose a pleasing dog dragged
   around us as we walked.
I think I remember: mother, sinking in
   the clay, carrying me across the
   wet fields. It is still far
   to the Russian lines.
I see: you, as you lecture, one foot
   out of shoe, rubbing the other.
I think (too much): of spin glass, spun,
   the signature of spins that can't
   be flipped, frustration frozen in, memory.

But all that is looking
glass empathy.
Doubt,
the surrogate demon,
whispers
this will not do
not today.

Nightmare

The steamed-up bathroom mirror resists
wiping with her terry towel. It will
not reflect her face. She persists, and her
determined, expert strokes clear it suddenly.
Uncovering a forest path, across which
stranded waves of brown pine needles guide
a horned advent of snails after rain.
She has to run—feels/hears the home-wrecking
squash. She freezes. A slimy snail
begins to crawl up her other leg. And
as she raises her eyes, the fox, black band
across his tan ears, quietly moves off
not in his smooth regal canter, but like
a cat that he isn't, bounding away.
She cannot run.
She cannot stand still,
and wakes to soft rain on her roof window.

Transeunt

Seemingly
substanceless air
through which the yellowing
afternoon light passes; chancily
moving air that gambles with gravity
to make the chestnuts knock-knock to the ground;
you
would seem
to deny the cluttering
of this aether by semipermanent
contrails of causality, control and intent,
the untended weft of events, past and imperfect
reaching,
filling the
quad with mind's eye
harpoon glances at girls'
legs, the substance of their tee shirt
legends, balls thrown hard then, frisbees floating yesterday
criss-
cross lines
of running, arms
outstretched to meet him,
knotted lines of evasion, robins'
low down worm hole lines intertwining
with now dormant angers' spherical firework bursts.
What was
empty is full
of frayed ribbons. And
someone else holds the scissors,
the broom, and reaches for the cleansing flame.

If Anger

If anger dissipates
    then into what?
On a beach red flotsam
jabbed by a stick,

underfoot the crunch
    of hermit crab shells,
stones skipped with malice,
for the splash.

Only a corporal of entropy?

This iron and jade phoenix,
ascending on the sooty trace
of mind's fire, wings
a claim to the
contrathermodynamic. So—

If anger accrues
    then from where?
The thicket of trip fuses—
traffic, unbalanced accounts,

a slippery cold "Yes, if
    you think it best."
Accelerator pedal
to the floor. Bleak sulk.

The stars go out once in a while
it's no big deal.

Sudan Fringe, 1985

People,
what *were* people,
lodged under trees, in tents,
from helicopters that pass timely
as the evening news, from
above, people,
fixed sand grains
blown into pitted limestone
nodules left by that older sea,
now reclaiming, diurnal
in kindling sand,
wind of another surge.

Rahel,
the dusted glisten
of your distended belly
pulses too quickly. Stretch marks;
your children doze, minds
still play at play,
drag sticks
through caked dirt,
scratch for roots, allium;
scatter to canyons, picking up tuft
headdresses of dried grass
soon snatched from them
for the fire.
The live, expectant
blades were scouted out
by imploded goats, all ribs,
as intent as the escarpment that
rises to dissect a dune.

Rahel
tries to stand,
the children's shirt rags
need scrubbing
with sand
to abrade
salt, dirt, grease,
the stiffening sense
of what the desert night
may bear away
and down
and in.

Modern Job

In Jerusalem the Lord waits,
in his temple, in the rubble of the earth.
Buried for centuries, watered by his people's tears,
cordoned off from his sacrifice,
the spirit waits.

In Auschwitz the trees flower,
swaying, under the dome of his sky.
Nourished, fertilized by the ashes and bones of believers,
beneficiary of the holocaust,
His greenery flowers.

In Hebron his folk pray—
side by side, the sons of Jacob and Esau.
Compartmented, divided by the wounds of their martyrs,
intransigent in their grief,
His minions pray.

Let him wait.
In the gene-lines of our poor people
let the strand of the messiah be denatured, lost and
        unduplicated.
He was silent in our need.
Now let him wait.

Doppelgänger

The black and white photo's point is Rosa,
twenty, in her first trench coat. Rosa in
Vienna, 1935, and she beams,
up on life, bundled in this coat, standing

a discreet space away from this larger-
than-life male nude of intersecting planes,
metallic softs, all shiny black. He turns
to the side, this monument to youth or (black

forgiven) a hint of Aryan art. This
representation Rosa graces, for she
is beautiful and her briefcase is stuffed
with Mann and general relativity.

Time frame shift. Fifty years pass, the print
with scalloped edges is pressed on
a visitor from Vienna. Here she was
happy, and the statue, does it stand?

The photograph—is it an affidavit
to having lived, or . . . a matte, prefigured
death? A precipitated moment
that was past just as it was, light

that bounded free now herded by lens
and focal plane shutter to silver
halide graininess. Light fixed, making
dark, inversion fitting imprisonment.

Then the printing bulb's glare, on to
another deception as we are made to see
white where there are no silver grains.
Space killed by flatness and time—well

a marker is set at $t = 0$, cleaving the slow
curve of before and after. Vienna cropped
to a woman and a statue; but the earth
moved, and people in brown shirts,

who were people, lift arms by the statue
and load trains bearing Rosas past barbed
wires to camps where no one needs cameras.

Topaz, Gomez et Cie.

The insouciance of the crowd made her tremble.
In faceted glasses champagne sparkled and flowed.
Garnets flashed in the dark, and fandangos
of light played with velvet gloves.
They were introduced, applauded.
  Topaz, Gomez et Cie.

She sang, she danced, he played.
The grin on his face was affixed with cement,
yet broken here and there in sweat and pimples.
The spotlight caught him, but it
could not arrest the trembling strings.
  Topaz, Gomez et Cie.

Turbot and crayfish, tortes piled on high.
Swirling voices, a song and then castanets,
breaking through the waterfall of polite conversation.
Clicks on a parquet floor, chairs scraping,
the crowd gathers, unwillingly.
  Topaz, Gomez et Cie.

The dancer sang of abandoned love,
of tents sprawled in the hot sun.
Her many-colored skirts rose in waves,
her back arched, in line with the stars.
Lost love, dangerous love, vendetta, and death.
  Topaz, Gomez et Cie.

Few heard her. No one saw him.
The elegant guests were there to coo
and admire the opulent spread,
to toast the bored bride,
to ask who was not yet dead.

The entertainment was bought
through an agency.
"Ah yes, they will be different.
They will provide fun, ambience,
a touch of the south.
Let us take them,
they're better than a dance band,
and a string quartet doesn't quite
fit the occasion.
How much? Oh, that's fine.
Laura will set a place for them in the kitchen."

Autumn Entelechies

1

The fever is past
but I feel fragile.
Like the Egyptian glass bottle of iridescent green,
      pasted together, but showing the cracks.
Like the Nabatean beads, peeling away sharp,
      onion-like, but corroded layers.
Like the old Coptic textile fragment, tattered
      and fading in all but its yellow and red.
I feel fragile.
My pieces are all there,
but they are held by weak ties.
My head feels the draft.
Mount me in the same museum case.
      Protect me from the wind.
            Arrange me and I will come to life again.

2

These are the days when the clouds
descend on our town. You see
them coming from our side.
The town is processed
by their passage, piecemeal
fabricated, pressed into existence.
Tree trunks made to be lost in the camouflage
of fall now jut before the fog.
That yellow house wasn't there before!
The glen's cleft protrudes.
A two dimensional curtain
focuses a plane

by obliterating the background.
Then, against your mind's
ever-conservative
wish
to freeze
that scene,
while you scan
it changes.

3

Things have such difficulty
in becoming . . . The restless
blackbirds in the trees there,
what makes them so?
Too easy for the toolmaker
in me to zoom in, dissect, and
in the end (or at least
where I choose to stop)
adduce—neat molecules,
restive, stochastically
colliding to fabricate
the biochemical tinkerer's
tool kit, with it to assemble,
in sublime bondage
to the anarchy that drives,
things—as simply
laid out as microscopic
barbs on feathers, even
what is built into the chatter
of obscured birds.
                    But that
will not do. A purpose must be
externally organized; here
the hunter's gun, shot scattering,
reverberations—afeared,

in cawing disarray, they assail
the space newly cleared by the leaves,
are strewn to the sky . . .
only, in sweet time
to wheel into the flock
that we demand them to be.

Early Seen

Sound-mixer
morning, knows
what to do with gutter
drip, chickadees' steep
high-low whistle dialog, silences
that need be and doves' distanter coo to blue.

Autodidact
morning, grays
mastered, tries for green
and there fails to hide the jag,
skew hung tilt of the apple tree branch,
a weighty curve
that split, not cleanly
in last night's storm.

Bring On Gene Kelly

We know that each one is different,
that the patenters have daydreamt
new ways to make us press here, slide

up there, trained us to doubt if
their creation will act out its internal
logic. This mechanism *will* work,

the metal tubes rise, ribs elbow
out radially, raising a dome
to the droopy sky, from which

it drips but doesn't pour yet—
but soon, soon—click.
The sail, which was not meant

to be a sail is in place.
Taut, quasi-waterproof fabric
to deflect the drippings from God's tail.

One umbrella, soft rain, riddle song:
Can two walk under and not touch,
the first brush of skin demanding more?

One umbrella, hard rain, ragged tune.
A couple, whose coat sleeves are
charged to repel with the recall of love
doused by this or that rain, by many rains.

Parasol, parapluie
   Men swinging it up to
   their shoulder, playing war
   tip-tapping the ground. Macho . . .
   but only if it's folded.

Parapluie, parasol
    Your push button release
    mechanism doesn't work
    today, boy.

Focusing lens for the wind's
rush, which shoves this fabric
and metal contraption its way.

More than one hand can take,
and the other has a heavy
briefcase. Bends and creaks.

And always the risk of inversion,
mangled spokes calling up
the textbooks of the ski-town doctor.

It's easy to forget
that parachutes can't fly up.

At their worst in crowds
creating protocols of tilting
and stretching as our

apparent volume increases.
At the least we're supposed
to stay dry. But as if

the waters' cycle were changed
by man, as if rain rose from
rivers, sewers and gutters,

my pants legs still get wet.

Allure of the Tepid

Dare a love that's static,
free of high and fast
discharges, ups, blue downs,
auction hammers, spending
binges and gossip's ammo.

We're not all screaming for love bite.

Dare just wavelets, dare
equilibrium—hot
water bottles, faded
photos, the said amiably
repeated. Then we'll swing,
but only in a hammock,
and mount the curve
of slow volition, to memory
of tea dancing, a Russian coin to wish on.

Three Japanese Edo-Period Pots

Bowl 1

Witness to old fire,
you beg to be picked up
and returned
to human hands.
And turned . . .
my controlled combustion
pressing warm life
into your creamy glaze
which, once viscously boiling
in 1629
congealed
into pocked perfection.

Bowl 2

Lead-glazed raku,
black, not just dark
but no less comely.
And the sheen of the
night kiln's fire is
in your smooth parts,
in your rough.
then . . . a cleft
through which the unglazed
clay, your solid soul
emerges.

Bowl 3

Three bands—mauve, gray, mauve.
In balanced contention the caught
but rising matte gray conspires
with the pot's rough rim
to ride me over the edge, where
I see the green froth of
ceremonial tea.

All three

You are not a circle, but its end,
the genteel force that makes us turn, turn, turn
in echo of your creation.
In flows of glaze, crackles ceramic,
dimples, burrs, ridges and scratches,
the way the ash fell,
textural evidence to chance.
Cultivated—I see heaps of shards—
imperfection, to reveal to refractory
man the perfection sought
in the potter's mind.

And now placed into my hands.
So few things in this world
were really meant to be held . . .

Before ever again I
call a rough object imperfect
I will remember Koetsu's bowls.

To Alexander Zholkovsky, in Exile in Los Angeles

Pre-post-structuralist Alik
wheels away from USC in
the morn, his sandals meld
with the pedals, this street
rolls his bicycle, steel shines on spokes.
Bearded Alik, in search of nude beaches.
Down to the sea, except it's not down
but straight, the hills in the distance
already hazy in the purple-brown
translucence of photochemical smog.
The sun is warm on his back, dyeing
away Ithaca winters. Alik
in unrainy Southern California
and he doesn't drive.

Cycle on, Pasternakian friend.
Cycle on, Alik, only thirty miles to the nearest beach.
They say the sands of Venice are pearly
and auburn girls crowd fabled Malibu.
If you long to see the surf of sainted Monica
do not be deterred, Alik
by the tar pits of La Brea
the muffler shops of Sepulveda Blvd.
Stop at the Church of the Spirit of Holy Monetarism,
detour for a semiotic analysis of El Segundo's
    taco shop signs.
There is no Penelope waiting at home . . .

Oh, Alik, have the Angeleno lotus-eaters
sated you with their buckthorn weed?
Buy yourself some chaps, with deerskin
fringes to blow in the wind as you ride, and
come home, Alik.

V

The Difference between Art and Science

—*for Jorge Calado*

From this Munch painting
of someone pained on a bridge,

hands held to ears, the observer
could scrape an orange

micron speck. He could
mount it on a slide, fine-tune

the fast beams that circle
under parking lots and football

fields, prodded on by magnets'
handless shove, focus, for that

is his craft, the probe particles
(fancy calibrated stones)

to jarring graphed impact
in the paint. The search

is for the force of the scream.
But the particles' pry is

too strong—they shock loose
the paint molecules, in sound

demonstration of the uncertainty
principle. The painting hangs;

Norwegian sky and harbor
pick up the scream, beam

it into the observer's skull.
There, echoing, effect change.

Cosmetic Company Buys Eisenhower College

*Much of this material is taken from the November
1983 issue of* Cosmetics and Toiletries.

Prettying our bodies, we mask
the poor times. The paint
is for the mirror, that pert two-
dimensional mock-up of a self
already uplifted. Then the blues
slough away, love comes, one
of several rises—well, why not
luxuriate and embellish?
The investment committee's report
on the beauty care industry, recession-
proof, smelled good. Approved.
They hired away the Vice-President
for Finance of Colgate-Palmolive,
three vets fresh out of Cornell,
a covey of formulators and perfumers
who mixed their first fragrance chords
at Helene Curtis. Eisenhower
College came cheaply—the science
labs, gym and kitchen, empty
three years, now watched incubators,
the limited color wheels of lip
glosses and pomades, burbling
pumps, centrifuges and magnetic
stirrers. White coat heaven.

The new lab head read poetry
which taught him, he said, we must
imitate nature. "How near," here he
shuffled his technical meeting
notes, "how near my ladies',

our customers', longed-for purple
nails, polish flake- and chip-
proof, how near those nails did
resemble the pier pilings to which
the marine mussel *Mytilus
edilus* adheres!" Out of a million
years good habit it oozes, ever
so effortlessly, a protein with Ala-Lys-
Pro-Ser-Tyr-Hyp-Hyp-Thr-
DOPA-Lys sequences, stuttered
seventy-five times (a reading loop
or lapse in the genetic code?) in this
polyphenolic protein. To bind, bind,
never to release in its salty life-
time. The mussels' secret is nearly
out, we only need fiddle
with the sequence a touch, then
engineer our own private reserve
E. coli strains to pour out
freight car lots. The under-
coating of the century is on its way.

One of the rehired buildings-
and-grounds people brought us
Aunt Brenda's recipe for rashes,
poison ivy, the rolling, falling kid
itches of summers. She would cook
up some oatmeal and spread
it on the skin. Marketing pointed
out that drugstores do not like
to sell old oatmeal, and so
our formulators, sequestered
in their converted kitchen until
our patent position is secure, boil
up steamy steel vats of oatmeal,
admix our secret ingredient, hops.
Homogenized, press-sieved, our

colloidal, anti-itching oatmeal
extract waits in plastic
jars for its trade name. Testing
is underway, but we don't
expect any trouble from the FDA.

Good things fall to the prepared
mind. By some German donor's
whim the Eisenhower College gym
was rich in steam baths. The new
Deodorant Division thought big:
Heated intact oxen discharged
sweat in a steady outpour for
a while, then fell into pulsed
patterns with five minute periodicities
synchronized animal to animal.
And I had to clean the floor
after them. Next door, in the erstwhile
shower stalls, isolated perfused
horse skin studies taught us
that adrenalin induced sweating.
So rare that one gets large
animal models for antiperspirants.

The No. 1 depilatory spot
is shared by Neet and Nair, but
we propose to pull past them
in this bushy market. Our lotion
contains calcium hydroxide,
calcium thioglycolate, sodium
silicate, mineral oil and an activated
alumina silicone product. If only
we could find a replacement
for two ingredients we could
label it as "all natural." Hypo-
allergenic, no offensive odor,
it smoothes away unwanted hair

in 5–10 minutes. Coarser hair
may take a bit longer. Our
desperate customers are advised
not to use it around the eyes,
inside nose or ears, or in peri-
anal and genital areas. But
legs, arms, underarms, face,
even bikini line will do.

Long lines of empty sinks,
tiled floors; the toilet stalls
had to be ripped up but the scene
was right for field tests of our
ultra-high foam dentifrice.
A heavy-bodied astringent
product, whipped-cream texture,
sweeps up and entraps food
particles, gum-line debris,
bacteria. Lines of volunteers
gargle, then brush their teeth
a canonical three minutes,
in harmonies of swishing
punctuated by timer beeps
and the forced expulsion
of water froths. By afternoon
they shape tentative claims
that the clocks cheat them,
slow to the side of eternity.
they lean with one hand
on the sink, snatch reflections
of their neighbors. The consensus
is for coconut flavor, but something,
something must be added
to discourage such wanton swallowing.

It took some disinfection, but
the gym lockers proved ideal

for raising adult female and castrated
male hamsters. A banner hung
from the roof: "Acne is the bane."
Before the females got testy,
into the pinna of both groups
we injected subcutaneously
Epidermal Growth Factor.
The number of cells per sebaceous
gland increased. The effect
was fortunately localized
to the treated ear and was
equally induced by the injection
of testosterone into that organ.
The hamster keeper's wife
reported weird bedroom games,
but we must do what
we can for the teenage boy.

"The art of expressing emotions"

"That lush, silken feel. Rich dense foam."

"Viscosity does it all"

"We came up with a pair of nonionics
that are really sweethearts"

"Proteins with personal appeal"

"Winning scents"

"A gel with an outstanding rheology"

"The essential oils and extracts of flowers,
leaves, roots, wood and musks"

". . . mix, blend, emulsify,
moisturize, add emolliency,
lubricate, bind, release."

She Sang

The air owed it to you. For those
many times it dove avidly
into your expanding chest. It knew

there would be organized, expelled
with the clarion impress of tone
and overtone. You did so much

for air that it had longed for—
to dance, with us, in Lillas Pastia's
tavern by the ramparts of Seville.

To stroke Tatiana's hair as she
writes to Onegin, even on that
dread hill to join you and the flute

draping Jesus down from our cross.
Then, the air was pleased to be your
errand boy, to pass and be passed

through by your pellucid song.
You pushed it on tactfully, you gave
it pause. Ungrateful aether, then,

for in the end, when air became
hard to come by, the uncoordinated
road gang strain of your mouth, tensed

neck and chest had to pry it out
in jagged blocks from a quarry
that we could not see. To be consumed

in one obliterating heave, with
aftershocks of gasping. No coda,
only that raspy dissonant summons

of a fickle accompanist.

Cavafy's Choice

A face. From smoky distance
or some dark, in slow-motion
acknowledgment of its nearing

the still androgynous image
collects itself. Proffered in sequence
are ambiguities of cut or sweep

of hair, curls, chin shadows,
silhouette of a shirt collar
or the sweet curve of its absence;

it is too dim or far yet for lips
or the telltale eye-cheek complex
to be seen. The expectant mind

awaits the spur of gender
choice to will down the prescored
nerves the imperative I-you

scan of softs that are or may be.
Or . . . the unsexed way in which
this Alexandrian skips over

the woman's face, searching
behind and through her for the
boy of the long hard night.

Red Alert Rag

I have to tell you
how we sat drinking beer—
Friday I think it was—
in Randy's place. Rain
outside, cats and dogs,
Just sheets of rain. Jerry
had this new bright crimson
jacket, he went out for another
case of beer, after we
collected the money.
The mood was right, relaxed,
we were getting high. Jerry
came back, all wet, and it
went on with the beer.
Such a great evening.
Manny told Jerry his
shirt was red on the shoulders
from the rain and the new
jacket running. I saw it too
and patches of red down his back.
"Incarnadine" I said.
Jerry sang out:
"Et incarnatus est."
It was fun.
"The carnage of
multitudinous carnations."
Manny got some sausage

and American cheese from
the fridge. Man, we were hungry.
"Eat meat in the cardinal's diner."
We laughed.
You can't believe how funny it was.
Jerry said: "I didn't know
Nadine had Inca blood,"
and Manny couldn't wait
to get in "I got to know
her in Macbeth's charnel house
chili parlor."
The cheese ran out, but
the beer did its work.
It was that kind of night.
I can't explain it
but the atmosphere was
just right, you know

Lift-to-Drag Ratios

Avjet feeds the ram
and thrust, thrust
and ram, a punch,
a path across

the sky. What a male
way to fly!
Look, softer lines
of geese, their

sequenced necks crimping
the sky, tie
to water and
tough landings

understood. The honk
drama of
a southering
traverse mends still

smarting sky. But in their
V I see
common principles
of flight apply.

An Unusual State of Matter

—for John M. Thomas

In the beach sands of Kerala,
abraded from the gneiss,
in the stream sands of North Carolina
one finds monazite, the solitary
mineral. In its crystalline beginning
there was order, there was a lattice.
And the atoms—cerium, lanthanum,
thorium, yttrium, phosphate—danced
round their predestined sites,
tethered by the massless springs
of electrostatics
and by their neighbors' bulk.
 They vibrated,
  and sang
   in quantized harmony
to absent listeners, to me.

But the enemy is within.
The radioactive thorium's
nervous nuclei explode
in the random thrum
 of a hammer
  of no Norse god.
The invisible searchlights
of hell, gamma rays,
flash down the lattice.
Alpha particles, crazed nuclear
debris, are thrust on megavolt
missions of chance destruction.
The remnant atom, transmuted, recoils,
freeing itself from its lattice point,
cannonballs awry through

a crowded dance floor.
There are no exits to run to.
In chain collisions of disruption
neighbors are knocked from their sites.
The crystal swells from once limpid
long-range, short-range order
to yellow-brown amorphousness.
Faults,
defects,
vacancies,
dislocations,
interstitials,
undefine the metamict state.

Photograph by Eva B. Hoffmann

About the Author

Roald Hoffmann was born in 1937 in Zloczow, then Poland, now the Soviet Union. After surviving the Nazi occupation and after several years of postwar wandering in Europe, he and his mother and stepfather made their way to the United States in 1949, settling in New York City. He graduated from Stuyvesant High School, Columbia University, and from Harvard University with an M.A. in physics and Ph.D. in chemical physics. Since 1965, Hoffmann has been engaged in teaching and research in theoretical chemistry at Cornell University, where he is now John A. Newman Professor of Physical Science.

Hoffmann's research interests are wide-ranging and his work has earned him numerous honors and awards, including the 1981 Nobel Prize in Chemistry, which he shared with Kenichi Fukui. Hoffmann is interested in the geometry and reactivity of molecules, in explaining from calculations of the motions of molecules' electrons why those molecules have the structures they do and why they react in specific ways. He likes to characterize as "applied theoretical chemistry" the particular blend of computations generated by experiment with the construction of generalized models that is his contribution to chemistry.

Hoffmann had his first real introduction to poetry at Columbia from Mark Van Doren, the great teacher and critic whose influence was at its height in the 1950s. Through the years Hoffmann has maintained his interest in literature, particularly German and Russian literature. He began to write poetry ten years ago, but it is only three years ago that his work began to be published. Hoffmann owes much to a poetry group at Cornell that includes A.R. Ammons, Phyllis Janowitz, and David Burak.